CAUGHT BETWEEN
A Rock and A Blessing

How to Get Through While Your Going Through

JOYCE Y. LEMMON

Published and distributed in the United States by Joyce Y. Lemmon, Long Island, New York

Copyright © 2021 by Joyce Y. Lemmon

All rights reserved. No parts of this book be reproduced by any mechanical, photographic, or electronic process, or in the form of phonographic recording; nor may it be stored in a retrieval system, transmitted, or otherwise be copied for public or private use – other than for "fair use" as brief quotations embodied in articles and reviews – without prior written permission of the publisher.

The author of this book does not dispense medical advice or prescribe any technique as a form of treatment for physical, emotional, or medical problems without the advice of a physician, either directly or indirectly. The author intends to offer information of a general nature to help you in your quest for emotional and spiritual well-being. If you use any of the information in this book for yourself, which is your constitutional right, the author or publisher assumes no responsibility for your actions.

All scripture references (KJV, MSG, NASB, NKJV, and NLT) can be found at www.biblegateway.com

Cover Design – Okomota

Editing and Layout – Pen Publish Profit, LLC and Robin E. Devonish

Interior Design – Istvan Szabo, Ifj., Sapphire Guardian International

Front and Back Cover Photo: JSR Photography

ISBN – 978-1-7377966-0-2

ACKNOWLEDGMENTS

I thank God for the opportunity and privilege to write this book. It is because of His mercy and grace that I live, move, and have my being.

My husband of 43 years, Elder Michael Lemmon, thank you for your encouragement and support, it's never unnoticed.

To my wonderful children Donniese, Andrea, Brandon, son-in-love Chad, and granddaughters Jeanelle, Siobhan, and Mikaela, you guys are my heartbeat and give me pure joy. I am so glad God blessed me with all of you.

My sisters Yvonne, Sheila, and Kim, thank you. You are so precious to me. You always believed in me even when I did not believe in myself.

My mother-in-love Mother Ollia Anderson; sisters-in-love Antoinette Anderson and Ana Anderson and brothers-in-love Antonio Anderson, Frank Webster, and Nestor Payne Sr. You have always encouraged and supported my endeavors. Thank You for being a tremendous blessing in my life.

My father in Durham, North Carolina, Mr. James Burgess. I love you.

Deliverance Tabernacle, you are the most incredible ministry on this side of heaven. You have given me so much joy. From the beginning, you had my back, and I pray that you all receive an abundance of blessings.

My dearest sister and brother in Christ, Apostle Patricia Wiley and Pastor Thomas Warren who never let up, reminding me that God was waiting on me to complete this assignment. I love you both, and may God continue to bless you.

My nieces, nephews, aunts, uncles, and entire family, I love you all to life.

To Sister Robin Devonish, thank you for your patience. You promised to annoy me, and I am grateful because I needed your persistence to complete this assignment.

Last, I would like to dedicate this accomplishment to the memory of my parents Ansel and Numa E. Watson. Words cannot express how much I miss you and wish you were both here to witness this achievement. I will love you for an eternity.

INTRODUCTION

There is an old saying, "I'm caught between a rock and a hard place." The statement indicates that an individual is in a position of indecisiveness. When not sure of what to do, making decisions becomes a dilemma. In these cases, the pros and cons are weighed, hoping to make the right or best decision.

Traveling this Christian journey for many years now, I've observed that we, believers in Christ, encounter many challenges and face obstacles or situations. Some issues are mind-boggling to the point of feeling uncertain or caught in the middle.

The scripture teaches us to leave everything in God's hands, trust him fully, and not lean to our understanding. However, when faced with adversity, we begin to experience anxiety, fear and feel like we must decide how to handle our current circumstances. We attempt to make sense of it all and can't. We become overwhelmed and anxious until we conclude that God has taken too long to come to our rescue. Our impatience moves us to take matters into our own hands and justify why we are interfering with God's timing of handling the situation. So now we're entangled and caught between what we are going through versus what God said.

I have experienced anxiety, fear, and being indecisive. Many times, I felt like God was taking too long to answer. I didn't know what to do. More times than I can count, I made the wrong decision. However, through my experiences, I have learned to encourage myself using various scriptures like:

> Isaiah 54:17a, "But in that coming day no weapon turned against you will succeed. You will silence every voice raised up to accuse you." (NLT)
>
> Mark 11:24, "I tell you, you can pray for anything, and if you believe that you've received it, it will be yours." (NLT)
>
> Hebrews 11:1 "The fundamental fact of existence is that this trust in God, this faith, is the firm foundation under everything that makes life worth living. It's our handle on what we can't see." (MSG)

If we were to be completely honest, those like me who preach the gospel, teach the scriptures and try to encourage other believers to hold on when they are faced with various challenges, is a lot sometimes. What happens when we pastors, preachers, and leaders, etc., are challenged with some of the same obstacles or situations? For example, we encourage others to hold on to their faith and trust God because he will supply all their needs (while for some leaders) lights are being turned off and we are the ones in jeopardy of losing a house or car. When pain, stress, uncertainty, and discomfort knock on our doors, we too begin to wonder how in the world we will get through it. Yes, as leaders, we too become a little shaky, and feel caught between that hard place and the blessings God promised us.

If you are a believer, I'm confident you've have felt those emotions and have been in places of pain, discomfort, and uncertainty. You were stuck between two spaces, fully believing God will fix it and attempted to wait on his promises.

Anyone who preaches or teaches never experiencing being in dilemmas or complex situations, I am inclined to believe dishonesty on their part. Every believer is challenged at some point in their life. Even the Apostle Paul in 2 Corinthians 12:7-8 said he had a thorn in his side and asked God to remove it three times. I'm certain that you've had a thorn. Maybe it wasn't like Paul's experience, but one that either made you want to change your mind about or want to quit ministry all together.

If you are a pastor or leader like me, you know that we sometimes become a little weary with our assignment, especially when preaching or trying to lead folk who just don't listen. We have a God assignment and sometimes wondered if it's worth the pain, the aggravation, and the YES! Was the call worth the thorn? We feel stuck between obedience and disobedience or what God told us to do versus what we prefer to do.

Paul wanted the pain and discomfort gone from his life so that he could be more effective. Having experienced pain, discomfort, and uncertainty, I can understand Paul's request. I have often been in a place where I asked the Lord to resolve many circumstances that seemed to be hindering me from flowing in my assignment.

I am also reminded of Jesus in the Garden of Gethsemane. In the scripture, it says, "He went a little farther and fell on His face and prayed, saying, "O my Father, if it be possible, let this cup pass from Me." (Matthew 26:39a – NKJV)

Jesus knew he had an assignment to fulfill, but for a moment, part of him did not want to go through with it. He was caught between doing his father's will versus no redemption or salvation for God's people. When the decision was made, Jesus concluded by saying, "nevertheless not as I will, but as You will." (Matthew 26:39b)

How did Paul or any of us get through our situation while going through it? Jesus responded by letting Paul and the rest of us know that his Grace was all we needed because his power worked best in our weakness. God constantly lets us know that his grace is enough to accomplish the purpose he has for us.

My prayer for you (the believer, ministry leader, pastor, or layperson) is that you will receive the necessary tools and further insight on how to press your way through life's varied and difficult circumstances.

I pray you are blessed, and while you may be "Caught Between a Rock and a Blessing," let the Lord show you How to Get Through While Going Through.

CONTENTS

Acknowledgments i
Introduction iii
Chapter One: I Got Somebody To Fight For Me 1
Chapter Two: He Catches You Before You Fall 9
Chapter Three: If God Did It Before, He Will Do
   It Again 15
Chapter Four: God Is Still With Us 25
Chapter Five: When You Come To Yourself 35
Chapter Six: Throw Your Net Back In 51
Chapter Seven: Speak Life and Encourage
   Yourself 57
Chapter Eight: When God Blinds Your Enemies .. 63
Chapter Nine: Everybody Can't Go 73
Chapter Ten: Just Wait 83
Conclusion 91

CHAPTER ONE

I GOT SOMEBODY TO FIGHT FOR ME

2 Chronicles 20:17 – "You won't have to lift a hand in this battle; just stand firm, Judah and Jerusalem, and watch God's saving work for you take shape. Don't be afraid, don't waver. March out boldly tomorrow – God is with you." (MSG)

While waiting on the Lord, the enemy uses the opportunity to make us afraid. He plans to convince us that God will not show up or come to our rescue in times of trouble. It is during our weakest moments that the enemy attempts to make his case to prove that God is not who he says he is.

The acronym for fear is <u>F</u>alse <u>E</u>vidence <u>A</u>ppearing <u>R</u>eal. Please understand this doesn't mean that what you are going through isn't real. I know the pain, the hard time, and whatever you are dealing with is real.

If I were to define each word, I would say: *false* means not genuine or misleading; *evidence* means testimony, *appearing* means to become visible and *real* is defined as not artificial.

So, when the enemy plants the seed of fear, he misleads us by giving testimony to something not genuine, thus making it appear real. In other words, because he knows our present struggle, he uses the opportunity to...

1. Twist God's word.
2. Plant fear and doubt.
3. Make us second guess what God can and will do.

In the third chapter of Genesis, Eve told the serpent what the Lord said about the consequences of eating from the tree. The serpent changed what God instructed and said, "You will not die, but your eyes will be opened, and you will be like God." What the serpent presented was misleading and caused both Eve and Adam to eat the forbidden fruit.

The enemy uses every chance he can to mislead us. It is like being sold a diamond that looks authentic and expensive until you look through a magnifying glass exposing its flaws. To the natural eye, the diamond looked real but was of no use. We must be careful not to let our circumstances shield us from knowing what is and isn't genuine.

In the opening scripture of this chapter, the word got back to King Jehoshaphat of Israel that a great multitude of (three large) armies were coming against them. He became afraid. Fear further caused the king to see the strength in the number of armies and potentially being defeated. For a moment, he didn't see the strength and power of God. King Jehoshaphat possibly felt like he was caught between trusting God and fearing the armies. After all, he was king and the leader of God's people who looked to him to do something about the upcoming situation.

Usually, when the believer is under pressure, they begin to feel trapped. For example, all the bills are due, lights are getting cut off, phone is being disconnected, car is about to be repossessed, and the list goes on. Everything becomes overwhelming, and we allow our circumstances to overpower us and appear stronger than the strength and ability of the God we serve. Hold on! Do not give up!

Caught Between a Rock and a Blessing

Remember, the enemy wants to get you off-track and lose focus, but somebody is fighting for you.

Initially, King Jehoshaphat may have been afraid, but he sought the Lord and went on a fast to hear a word from Him. No matter how hard the situation appears or how frightened you feel, when you trust and seek God, He will give you an answer and directions to follow.

What was the result of this biblical story? A prophet named Jahaziel stood and spoke to the people of Judah. The first thing the prophet said was not to be afraid of the great multitude (20:15).

When we get attacked, it is usually a chain of financial, health, or family issues. If or when you are faced with any of those issues, the first thing to tackle is the spirit of fear. The Apostle Paul told Timothy - "For God has not given us a spirit of fear and timidity, but of power, love, and self-discipline." (2 Timothy 1:7 – NLT)

In their case, the enemy presented a situation where victory seemed impossible. Yes, the armies were coming but conquering God's people was never going to happen. God is bigger than any of our problems or circumstances. He is here to fight for us.

Once it was determined that they did not have to be afraid, the second thing Jahaziel did was give instructions on how to defeat the enemy. I believe that the same goes for Christ-followers today. Focus and don't allow the enemy to side-track us. We will hear God and receive our instructions for victory. What is so amazing about defeating the enemy, we never have to exert our energy to win. The Lord told the people through his prophet that the battle was not theirs but his. That statement alone is comforting. To know that we don't have to fight, or worry is such a relief.

My Personal Application

As a child, I never liked fighting. I was quiet and always had my nose in my schoolwork. I didn't involve myself in quarrels with the other kids. All I wanted was good grades. My studious ways caused other problems. I was called the "teacher's pet," "brainiac," and other choice words.

Then the day came when the class bully Richard wanted to terrorize me. When school ended, and it was time to exit the building, he stood in front of the door and refused to let me leave. Honestly, I was afraid. I didn't know how to stand up to him and feared telling anyone because of what he might do. I didn't even tell my mother, who was standing at the corner waiting for me. She couldn't understand why I was always the last one out of school. She thought I was playing inside the building. I felt trapped with nowhere to go.

After several weeks of mental torture, I decided enough was enough. I was tired of getting into trouble for being late. I had to deal with the fear. Not knowing what would happen, and because he was a scary kid, I had to figure something out. I was young, but I remember asking God to help me. There was a sense of strength that covered me, and I felt confident that God could do it if I just prayed and asked him.

The next day I arrived at school, the teacher told us that Richard would no longer be in our class or school because his family was moving to the Bronx. I guess you can say that was the first time I experienced God answering my prayer. After hearing the news, I knew God came to my rescue. He fought for me without my having to do anything or tell anyone.

The Revelation

That's what happened with King Jehoshaphat. Seek the Lord + Declare a fast (Pray) = Receiving instructions to defeat the enemy.

The praise singers were placed out front to sing praises to God. For me, the key to my victory was to seek and trust God to act on my behalf. When the word came that Judah was about to be invaded by three different armies, who would have thought that something as simple as praise and worship would be the key to Judah's victory? Their act of praise not only resulted in triumph, but they also received an abundance of wealth which took three days to gather and collect. Just know that whenever you **Praise** God, you **Raise** Him.

In other words, praise is a word that, when put into action, something had to happen. Just singing "Praise the Lord for His mercy endures forever" (vs. 21) destroyed three armies without Judah ever lifting a weapon against them. God did it all. The Lord God caused the enemies to fight amongst themselves. When they became confused, they all perished.

I never had to fight Richard the bully. I prayed for help and God fought for me. When the Prophet

Caught Between a Rock and a Blessing

Jahaziel stood before the people and told them that the fight belonged to God, they never lifted their swords. I encourage you to use the tool of praise in your mouth, and God will do the rest.

CHAPTER TWO

HE CATCHES YOU BEFORE YOU FALL

Jude vs. 24 – "Now unto him that is able to keep you from falling, and to present you faultless before the presence of his glory with exceeding joy." (KJV)

Have you ever played the game where you close your eyes and fall back, expecting the person standing behind to catch you before you hit the ground? Well, if you have, then you know it takes a great amount of trust on your part to believe the person/friend/associate will not let you fall and cause possible harm to you. As you are falling, you find yourself at peace, knowing that everything will be alright, and there are no doubts about the catcher.

The same applies when trying to figure out how to get through your situation while going through.

Caught Between a Rock and a Blessing

Believe the Lord will catch you before you fall! The trust and faith you had in the person standing behind you is the same trust and faith you need in God. Remember that he stands with you all the time. When going through trials, we tend to stop trusting God. We say that we can't feel his presence, or we wonder if he's nearby. We are distressed and feel like we are on a cliff edge or have come to a dead end with nowhere to go.

<u>My Personal Application</u>

I remember some years ago when my husband and I were in jeopardy of losing our home. We had a child away in college and were raising two at home. The mortgage company was constantly calling, which only intensified the anxiety. Fear was ever-present. A certain amount of payment was required to stop foreclosure proceedings. The amount needed wasn't available. I felt on the cliffs edge and looking at a dead end. Not knowing what to do, like the game, I closed my eyes, prayed, and trusted that God would keep us from falling.

Just when I felt no hope in this impossible dead-end situation, the phone rang. Keep in mind, no one knew about our circumstances. We never discussed it with anyone. When I answered the phone, on the other end were some individuals whom the Holy Spirit told them we needed help. God sent them to help and keep us from falling.

The Revelation

Isn't that how the children of Israel felt when they arrived at the Red Sea and asked Moses why they were brought to a place of emptiness with no return. As far as they were concerned, there were enough graves in Egypt to die there. (Exodus 14:11)

Sometimes I feel that God brings us to an edge in life to see if we truly trust Him. The edge is where we may experience the same hesitation felt when we closed our eyes and fell back, hoping God would catch us before hitting destruction.

For many generations, the children of Israel prayed for a deliverer, and God provided one through Moses. They came out of Egypt a free people only to hit a dead end, or so they thought.

As the story goes, they were standing at the edge of the Red Sea, (in FEAR) stressed.

Israel was caught between a rock (the enemy) and the blessing (the other side of the red sea),

Caught Between a Rock and a Blessing

---

with only the pillar of fire separating them. Pharaoh's army (Egyptians) was close on their heels. With nowhere to go except the raging sea, what would become of them and what would they do? When they were about to give up on any chance of escape, the path was made amid the sea, representing deep impossibilities.

How many times have you faced situations that seemed virtually impossible, and God made a way for escape? At the edge is where it seems that God does His best work. With nowhere to go, God made a path for them in the middle of the impossible. "With men, it is impossible, but not with God: for with God all things are possible." (Mark 10:27 KJV)

God caught them, and likewise, He catches us in the middle of impossible situations. We won't fall!

The story is another example of the rock and the blessing. Depending on the severity of the problem, we may try to fix it and not trust God. A part of us knows that God will come through, but another part of us will say we can't afford to wait that long. Again, this is the enemy's way of implementing the "fear factor." The temptation to personally handle matters is expected. Still, the Apostle Paul says, "No temptation has overtaken you, but such as is common to man; and God is faithful, who will not allow you to be tempted beyond what you are able, but with the temptation will provide the way of escape also, that you will be able to endure it." (1 Corinthians 10:13 – NASB)

In other words, God will not cause us to endure or be tempted by anything that may overtake us. He will provide a way out that will help us to endure it. We may not always escape the temptation, but when it is all over, we will be intact.

Jude says in verse 24 that he is able (has sufficient power, skill, or resources) to keep us from falling (stumbling). It is not God's desire that we fall but that he presents us faultless (unblameable and unreprovable) in his presence. That is why when we feel caught in the place of discomfort or distress that we look to the Lord who can keep us. Again, the Lord will catch you before you fall.

After the Lord has caught or prevented us from falling, a sense of joy comes. Jude implies in verse 24 that God experiences exceeding joy when he keeps us from stumbling and presents us faultless

Caught Between a Rock and a Blessing

in His presence. I interpret this as God being satisfied. I repeat it is not His desire that we fall. I do believe that when we trust God, He is given both joy and satisfaction. The Bible says that "without faith it is impossible to please him: for he that comes to God must believe that he is and that he is a rewarder of them that diligently seek him." (Hebrews 11:6)

Knowing that we trust and believe in him pleases him. Not only is God satisfied, but we are satisfied knowing that we have someone who stands with us to keep us from hurting ourselves. He is the one who will be there to assure us that he will never leave when we are afraid or feel trapped. On your next trial, try closing your eyes, trust God and lean back. He is standing there behind you with His hands and arms stretched out to catch you before you fall.

CHAPTER THREE

IF GOD DID IT BEFORE, HE WILL DO IT AGAIN

Mark 6:42-44 – "So they all are and were filled. And they took up twelve baskets full of the fragments, and of the fishes. Now those who had eaten the loaves were about five thousand men." (NKJV)

It seems that no matter how many times God brought us out of a situation, we doubt or fear whether he will free us from the next one. I don't know if it's because we think our next dilemma is far greater than the last, or it just seems too impossible to fix.

One illustration of this would be the numerous times that God delivered the children of Israel out of impossible situations.

1. The exit out of Egypt and the crossing of the Red Sea on dry land. (Exodus 14:21-22)

Caught Between a Rock and a Blessing

2. When they murmured and complained about not having any water, God turned the bitter water of Marah into sweet water so that they may drink (Exodus 1:22-25) and subsequently bringing them to a place called Elim where there are twelve wells of water (vs. 27).

3. While in the wilderness of sin, they again complained about needing bread, and the Lord provided manna, which meant "what is it" that was to be eaten, leaving none for the next day (Exodus 16:15). However, due to their lack of faith plus disobedience and the fear that they may not receive any more, they kept some manna until morning, which began to stink and become covered with worms yet again, leaving them with nothing to eat.

But guess what, saints? We are no different. How many times have we been given specific instructions to do something but did the total opposite because we thought God was not going to show up? Or we felt our dilemma was far greater than the last one and ultimately too impossible to fix? How many rough times have we had, and God brought us through victoriously, despite our unbelief?

Another example of God coming to someone's rescue more than once is with his servant David, the man after God's own heart. David experienced God coming to his rescue on several occasions.

1. From David's victorious battle with Goliath. (1 Samuel 17:40-54)
2. The times' Saul failed attempts to kill him because of jealousy. (1 Samuel 18:10-16)
3. When David pretended to be insane to preserve his life. (1 Samuel 21:10-15)

In every situation with David, the Lord proved that his blessings and help were on repeat.

No matter how many times we find ourselves caught in a place of discomfort and uncertainty but looking toward the promises and blessings of God, the enemy continues to whisper seeds of doubt that God will do it. The enemy will say things like, "this time God isn't coming to help" or "he already helped you out once." He will even tell us that God is tired of us asking him for help; the never-ending discouragement continues.

My Personal Application

I have been in some rough spots I thought would make me lose my mind. I remember wanting to sleep so I wouldn't have to face life's challenges. I would wake up and then force myself to go back to sleep, hoping the next time I awoke, things would be different. However, they were the same! Many told me to hold on because the Lord was going to see about me. In all honesty, the pain and discomfort of what I was going through were unbearable. I just wanted the problem to go away.

Please understand that I knew what God had done for me in the past and his capabilities. However, there I was, in the middle asking myself how I would get through the moment. I was reminded of the scripture where visitors came to Abraham's home and told him that his wife would have a son.

When Sarah laughed because she knew she was too old, one of the visitors asked, "Is anything too hard for the Lord?" (Genesis 18:14)

Keeping that question in my mind, I held on to my faith. I kept praying until the day God showed up. He made ways, and things began to improve. I did not become rich, but my bills were paid on time. My credit score began to increase, and I received a job promotion. I also accomplished what I wanted and prayed for, which was to be a blessing to others. For four years, I felt good, but then something happened. My life took a turn that put me back into that place of pain, discomfort, and stress.

While working my full-time job, the promotion I received was a management position. I was over several areas, one of which dealt with large amounts of money. One day after conducting my daily count, I discovered that over twenty-nine thousand dollars disappeared. The person responsible for the funds was out due to a family situation. I did everything I could to find the error. I later discovered that the money was stolen. An investigation ensued. I was never suspected of theft. However, because I was the manager in charge, I was held responsible for someone else's indiscretion that cost me my promotion and a large percentage of my salary. The ordeal affected me mentally and impacted my finances significantly. Everything that could go wrong did. My health suffered, and my faith decreased slightly.

A small part of me was convinced that God was not going to get me out of it. I questioned the Father to see if I had done something wrong to offend Him. How could this happen to me yet again? I felt trapped in a hole, and no one could hear me cry out for help. Where was God this time? I was innocent of the crime committed, so why wasn't he helping me?

However, despite the dilemma, I began to preach harder while shedding many tears. I was angry, but God still gave me a prophetic word to utter. At times I felt out of place, but the anointing on my life seemed to increase. I never really understood why I had to go through that, but when God finished bringing me through the storm, he restored me with a new promotion, salary increase, and most importantly, a stronger ministry.

The Revelation

In the Bible, the feeding of four thousand was not Jesus' first act of providing food for a great multitude with little resources; he had previously fed five thousand. Whatever God does, it's not a once-in-a-lifetime ability. He is an infinite God who can keep blessing us repeatedly.

In the gospel of Mark chapters six and eight, there are similarities regarding the feeding of the multitude. What is interesting about both chapters? The disciples questioned how so many people could be nutritionally satisfied, especially in the middle of the wilderness or desert place? Not understanding where the food supply was coming from to accommodate such a crowd, they wanted the people to go home and eat. Because the situation is enormous or seems impossible does not mean that God cannot handle it. That is the same understanding we must come to. God is grander than any situation that comes before us.

Again, remember that fear is False Evidence Appearing Real, but **"Now faith is the assurance of things hoped for, the conviction of things not seen."** (Hebrews 11:1 – NASB)

Indeed, if God fed five thousand, He could feed four thousand.

Saints of the Most High God, we must stop putting God in a box and understand a few things I'm sure we've heard before but bears repeating.

1. It is impossible to place limitations on the limitless one.
2. There is no beginning or end to him, only omnipresence, omniscience, and omnipotence!
3. God always accomplishes more than we might ask or think, according to the power that works in us. (Ephesians 3:20)
4. He does not do exceeding and then do abundantly but exceeds the already abundant by going over the top for us.

Now that we have this reminder, all we need to do is exercise the power that he has given by putting our trust and faith into action.

For me, this means, though I had intense pain in the storm and was stripped of a promotion through no fault of my own, Joel 2:25 says, God can restore everything that the cankerworm, the locust, and the palmerworm destroyed.

In the book of Job, we know that Job was an upright man who feared God and hated evil. It was Satan's request to challenge Job's standing in God. Upon being granted, Job lost everything he had. Did he curse God? No, but concluded, "God might kill me, but I have no other hope. I am going to argue my case with him." (Job 13:15 – NLT)

IF GOD DID IT BEFORE, I KNOW THAT HE WILL DO IT AGAIN.

CHAPTER FOUR

GOD IS STILL WITH US

Matthew 1:22-23 – "All of this occurred to fulfill the Lord's message through his prophet: Look! The virgin will conceive a child! She will give birth to a son, and they will call him Immanuel, which means "God is with us." (NLT)

This story about the conception and birth of our savior is remarkable. Whenever I think about this young virgin girl who became pregnant without ever knowing a man, I wonder what if it had been one of us. Would we have trusted God enough to withstand the ridicule? Would we have run away or hidden from our family and friends? How would we explain this, and who would believe us if we did?

In the previous verse (that opens this chapter) in Matthew, the writer tells us that the child's name would be called Jesus, which means "Yehoshua" or

"Jehovah saves." The name gives us his purpose for coming into the world. However, Immanuel means the Lord has come to live with us, reside, and dwell among us. John 1:14 says, "And the Word was made flesh, and dwelt among us, (and we beheld his glory, the glory as of the only begotten of the Father,) full of grace and truth."

Again, just imagine yourself as Mary, not looking or asking for anything, engaged to be married, innocently minding your business. Suddenly, God chooses you to carry out a unique assignment. The moment puts you in a position where you don't know how you got there, but you are. Or try and imagine yourself as Moses, lured to a mountain. Nothing is around but a burning bush that speaks with the authoritative voice of God, providing instruction of going back to Egypt to deliver the people from bondage.

Moses felt inadequate and asked God who he was to go before Pharaoh and deliver the children of Israel out of Egypt (Exodus 3:11). But God said to Moses in verse 12a, "Certainly I will be with you." (NASB)

When the Lord tells us that He is with us, we can take it to the bank. David said that he had never seen the righteous forsaken nor his seed begging bread (Psalm 37:25).

Just as Mary was chosen to bring forth or birth the savior into this world, we are selected to become pregnant and bring forth the ministry that lies within us. There goes the rock and the blessing again. You are caught between the promises of the Lord, giving birth to something unique and peculiar. Also, possible ridicule from your family, friends, and your church for stepping out in boldness and doing what God has instructed.

A young woman who finds herself pregnant and not married will ask herself, what do I do now? She knows for the next nine months, she will face several changes physically, mentally, emotionally, and even spiritually. Some of these changes she has no desire to encounter, like weight gain, getting sick, the inability to hang with her friends, and so forth. Then there is the anticipation of wanting to know if it is a boy or girl; who will the baby look like? I know for myself that I, too, wanted to know these things.

Well, when we are impregnated with a ministry like the young woman, there are some things we would rather not deal with. The commitment to study, responsibility, accountability to the assignment, and sometimes giving up things we like to do (party, social drinking, etc.) are a few. Becoming pregnant with ministry was not exactly on our "to-do list," and we had other plans. So, we ask God the infamous question – why me, Lord, only for Him to counter ask, why not you?

There are times when the Lord gives us another assignment after we just became comfortable with the previous project. In other words, it is like finding out you are pregnant again with your 2nd child when your first is still in diapers.

My Personal Application

I remember when the Lord called me to Pastor. At the time, I had been preaching for about seven years in my local church under my late Pastor, Elder Edward McCall. I had advanced to head organist. I was also an assistant organist for one of the subsidiaries within the Diocese. I was comfortable in my position and earning a salary. In addition to being a musician, I had the opportunity to preach at several ministries throughout the city and abroad. I became content and did not feel any pressure. BUT THEN THE CALL CAME! I knew it was God instructing me to launch out into the deep even though I didn't want to believe it.

Fear crept in because I was pregnant with something that seemed impossible at the time. I was given this tremendous responsibility to lead God's people. How was I going to start? Where was I going? Who was going with me? These were just a few questions I had on my mind. I was married with three young children and was concerned about putting them in a challenging situation.

There I was, a young black woman attempting to venture out as a Pastor. It was bad enough being a female preacher, but folk had pretty much accepted that. Being a pastor? Well, that was a horse of a different color. I didn't want to tell anyone. Even when I told my mother, who has since gone on to be with the Lord, I could sense the concern she had for me. Then there were those individuals I did mention it to, and some didn't think it was possible. I would get responses like, are you sure or why are you leaving the church? All I knew was, here I am, pregnant with something without a clue. How would I carry this baby to full term and subsequently give life to it?

Any woman who has ever given birth knows that there are stages to pregnancy called Trimesters. There are three of them, and each consists of three months. In each trimester, something different happens. For the first trimester, a woman may encounter morning sickness and mood swings. In the second trimester, she will experience fluttering or movement from the baby and some weight gain. Finally, during the last trimester, the woman begins to feel more tired, the need to visit the bathroom frequently, the movement of the baby increases, and ultimately labor results in the birth of a son or daughter.

When we become pregnant with ministry, we will also experience the different stages of its development. First, we must accept that we are pregnant, which will result in many feelings and anxieties. We will deal with the ups, downs, and frustration that accompany the ministry. As we go further along, we find ourselves being stretched and uncomfortable. We may experience mood swings, and part of us may desire for God to annul what he has given us. Even in nervousness and fear of what God has assigned, the one thing a pregnant woman, in the natural or spiritual, does not want is premature birth. In ministry, anything birthed before time is premature. The reason why a woman must endure nine months is to ensure that the baby she carries has sufficient time for development. Babies born ahead of time will likely spend time in an incubator due to the non-development of lungs or other body parts. Likewise, a ministry born too early will have more difficulty surviving than one of maturity.

When it is time to push or give birth to the ministry, it can be excruciating. Even in the final stage, when delivery is at hand, the doctor sometimes will have the mother stop pushing to ensure the umbilical cord is not wrapped around the baby's neck. Well, the enemy does not want us to birth our ministries. He does everything necessary to cause a malfunction. It is the enemy's primary purpose to suffocate what God is about to bring forth. He attempts to wrap a cord around the neck, hoping to kill or cause a "stillbirth." When the enemy tries to destroy, God steps in to ensure that nothing hinders the birth. Like the father who stays around to hold his wife's hand, God stays with us through the entire process.

The Revelation

When Joseph discovered that Mary was with child, he decided to put her away privately. When Moses encountered the burning bush and instructions to bring the children of Israel out of Egypt, the Lord told both not to be afraid. He was with them. Basically, God told me the same thing. He promised to be there. October 6, 1996, Deliverance Tabernacle was born. Besides, I was not alone. God sent people (congregants) with me. Despite some negativity, after nearly 25 years, we are still here.

The Apostle Paul said that we are more than conquerors and, "With God on our side like this, how can we lose?" (Romans 8:31 – MSG)

When pregnant with ministry, you will ask yourself, can I do this? I want to tell God, yes, but I am not sure if I am ready. How do I get to the finish line with everything that is going on in my life?

You will feel awkward, inconvenienced, uncomfortable, and won't seem to fit in with everyone else.

Remember, this was not an ideal situation for Mary, but the angel of the Lord said, "Don't be afraid, Mary the angel told her, for you have found favor with God." (Luke 1:30 – NLT)

We, too, have found favor with God, and we shall give birth regardless of how it looks because GOD IS WITH US!

CHAPTER FIVE

WHEN YOU COME TO YOURSELF

Luke 15:17 – "And when he came to himself, he said, How many of my father's hired servants have bread enough and to spare and I perish with hunger!" (KJV)

This chapter of Luke's gospel is where we find the parable of the lost or prodigal son recorded. He received his inheritance early, squandered it, became destitute, and returned home to a father with open arms. Though all of this is true, let us examine this biblical story a little closer.

Here is a man with two sons, and it is evident that he is well off and had made provision for them upon his passing. As a point of reference, please note that it was customary for the elder son to receive a double portion of the estate in the event of the father's death, leaving the youngest son one-third. However, this was not the case in this parable.

Caught Between a Rock and a Blessing

In this story, the younger son asked for his portion ahead of time and received it. Now, this was quite disrespectful, but his father obliged. If we were to stop there, I believe the questions would be:

1. Why did the father give it to him?
2. Why didn't his father just tell him no?
3. Why wasn't he reprimanded for being disrespectful because it wasn't time?

Before addressing the questions, just think where you or I asked for something that we should not have received because it was before its' time. But we accepted it anyway. For example, do you remember asking your mother for a cookie right before dinner, and she said no because it would ruin your appetite? However, we kept on asking, and she gave it, knowing the outcome of not finishing the dinner. Or do you remember asking and praying to God for something that we probably should have waited a little longer for (car, house, etc.)? He allowed us to receive it, resulting in a struggle to make mortgage or car payments. Of course, the answer is yes. We have often found ourselves in this situation.

There were other times when we got what we wanted but became angry or upset with our parents because things didn't go the way we wanted or expected. Yes, we became upset with God and threw blame for our mishaps. We had these emotions simply because we felt our parents or God should have known better. They could have insisted that we not pursue the "thing" we wanted or desired. So, after everything began to spiral out of control, it became their fault we were suffering or going through.

I, however, find that one reason we end up in situations like this is because during the begging and pleading, we didn't about the possible outcome. At that moment, nothing mattered. It was all about us, what we wanted or had to have.

My Personal Application

I remember when I had only been preaching for a couple of years. I was never rude or disobedient, but there was one time when I crossed the line. I was asked to preach an afternoon service at my local church. When the outline and information were brought to my pastor, he said no. Well, I could not understand why he would say no, especially when it was at our church, and he would be present. He, however, stuck to his decision of not letting me preach for that service. I became distraught and defiant. I even had an attitude and told him (my Pastor) he was wrong. I had preached a few times, and the spirit of the Lord moved mightily. People wanted to hear from me more. This is where becoming "puffed up" and I got a bit beside myself. When my pastor said I couldn't preach for the service, I felt like he didn't get the memo about how good people thought I was. How could he tell me no? However, I soon realized my behavior wasn't a good move. I quickly found out that when you go against your leader's decision, things will not work out for you in a positive way. I am here to let you know that it is one thing when you get a scolding from your parents, but when God scolds you: it's on a different level. In my case, God fixed it where no one asked me to minister. I quickly had to get over myself and get it together.

That is just what happened to the younger son. The Bible says in Luke 15:13, as soon as he "gathered all together," which means he turned all his assets into cash, he left home and wasted all of it. He had money and thought "he was the man" who could do it all. He probably had friends who loved spending and never imagined the money would run out. Does this remind you of anything? What did you continuously ask God for that was not in His perfect will for your life?

I have been there before, and needless to say, it's not fun. Being stuck on yourself causes a lot of problems. When you start thinking the world revolves around you or believe you are the best thing since chocolate cake, you've just created an unpleasant situation.

The Apostle Paul often warned us of being "puffed up" or too proud (1 Cor. Chapter 4). This form of vanity often leads to self-destruction. Proverbs 16:18 states, "Pride goes before destruction, and a haughty spirit before a fall." (NKJV)

Failure to come to yourself risks the chance of stumbling and ultimate destruction.

If I could have a sidebar for a moment, this is what I feel is happening within the body of Christ right now. Some men and women who have just entered ministry are becoming "full of themselves." They are shipwrecking by moving too fast and not taking time to mature. Somebody told them they were great and should start a ministry. They find themselves listening to people instead of listening to the Lord or their leaders. They only know two or three verses of scripture but have a laundry list of demands for them to come and minister at your church. Luke 10:7b, "for the laborer is worthy of his wages." (NKJV)

Becoming an effective orator of the gospel takes time and study. 2 Timothy 2:15 tells us, "Concentrate on doing your best for God, work you won't be ashamed of, laying out the truth plain and simple." (MSG)

The Revelation

The younger son ran out of his inheritance, money, and friends. He found himself joining a country that was not his own, eating foods (slop) that would have never crossed his dinner table at home.

You remember when we became teenagers and thought we knew everything? We believed we had it together, and mama and daddy knew nothing! Our parents told us, "You are smelling yourself," which meant we were becoming too grown. They reminded us how good we had it. Well, this is what happened to the youngest son. A know it all, he thought he was ready and entitled to his inheritance. No one could tell him otherwise. However, as he was feeding the swine, he had a revelation, came to himself, and realized how good he had it at home. The situation was preventable only if he would have waited for his time and turn.

Hungry and willing to eat the husks that the pigs were eating, the young man recalled how many servants were back at his father's house and how he had round-the-clock room attention. He realized who he was, and the blessings previously afforded to him.

When I realized that my pastor was partly responsible for my destiny, I came to myself, and never again did I disobey him even if I thought he was wrong. If you think you are so great of a preacher that you can have your own ministry, please re-think that decision before you plunge. Do not get stuck on yourself and become "puffed up" thinking you have arrived because if you do, you may experience what the youngest son experienced. You may find yourself lost, alone, and going through an almost impossible situation.

As we know, the youngest son came to himself, returned home, and was greeted by his father, who opened his arms and received him back with the giving of clothing, jewelry, food, and love. There was a feast and grand celebration. However, what about the elder son? Let us explore that a little further.

Luke 15:25-30 – "Now his older son was in the field, and when he came and approached the house, he heard music and dancing. And he summoned one of the servants and began inquiring what these things might be. And he said your brother has come, and your father has killed the fattened calf because he has received him back safe and sound. But he became angry and not willing to go in, and his father came out and began entreating him. But he answered and said to his father, Look! For many years I have been serving you, and I have never neglected a command of yours; and yet you have never given me a kid that I might be merry with my friends; but when this son of yours came, who has devoured your wealth with harlots, you killed the fattened calf for him." (NASB)

If every believer in Christ were honest, we can all attest to having felt like the elder son at some point during our Christian walk. Since becoming saved, we've tried to live according to the word and command of God. Most of us are or at least try to remain faithful regarding our service to the Lord and our church. We attend Bible study, sing on choirs, usher, and do everything asked of us. We are taught to give our tithes and offerings even when living paycheck to paycheck. When bills accumulate, we are taught to trust God to make a way. However, we watch as others who seemingly don't care or are uncommitted do whatever they want and appear to reap many blessings. We, the faithful, loyal, and committed, may desire to be like the others who receive the blessings we feel they're not worthy of. For a moment, we may consider giving up the "saved" or "church thing." Why bother? Our thought process becomes either I continue doing what is right; remain faithful and committed to my service for the Lord and the church, possibly without any type of reward or recognition. Or I can be like everyone else who appears to do whatever they want but still receives blessings.

This moment reminds me of a child who does well in school and obeys their parent but never receives those expensive pair of sneakers they asked for. Meanwhile, they see their peer do the complete opposite. That child has poor grades, is disobedient, yet they walk around with the name-brand sneakers and outfits. The child who does what's right would see rewarding that type of student as unfair. They may entertain the thought of acting just like the disobedient child.

Isn't that how the elder son felt? When you look at the story, he is in the field working and sweating. There was a party going on at the house. He wasn't invited or aware of the celebration, *and the party was at his house.* No one came and told him anything. It was not until he walked toward the house that he heard the music and inquired with one of the servants about what was going on. He discovered there was a celebration in honor of his youngest brother (Luke 15:25-30).

Now just imagine that happening to you or me. I don't know about you, but I believe I would have felt some type of way or became a little enraged. How are you having a party at my house and never told me? Not only are you having a party in the place where I live, but the party is for someone who has shown nothing but disrespect and disloyalty. The elder son became angry when he learned the party was for his brother. He was so mad; the Bible says he would not go inside (verse 28).

Have you ever been there before? I know I have. At one point, you became discouraged because everything you poured into ministry appeared to go unnoticed. You possibly thought, "Where is my blessing or my breakthrough?" You began to look at others being blessed. You felt they were far less deserving. You began thinking, maybe I should be like them. Your thoughts became wedged between doing your own thing or receiving the blessing for living right and serving the Lord.

We know that the elder son was in a position of receiving a double blessing upon his father's death. He knew that his inheritance would be great. But even with him knowing the outcome once his father passed, the special treatment his brother received bothered him.

After the elder son refused to enter the house, his father went out to speak to him. The son took the opportunity to express his feelings. He pointed out how for many years, he served his father faithfully. He never did anything wrong against him or disrespected the family. He continued to state how gratitude was never shown towards him, neither had he ever had a fun gathering with his friends. He further pointed out that as soon as the younger son, who was away doing whatever he wanted, came back home broke after living unrighteous. Not any calf, the fattest calf, fine clothing, and a ring were given to him. The youngest son completely messed up his life but is celebrated, an opportunity the elder son never had. Reading those few verses would probably have you siding with the elder son.

I think about individuals I admire, like Bishop TD Jakes and Mr. Steve Harvey, who in their lifetime endured some hardship before receiving their blessings. I've heard both men speak about struggling while remaining faithful to God. For example, the deacons at Bishop Jakes' church would take his beaten-up car and park it in the back of the church so no one would know it belonged to the pastor. His wife would wash and press his suit so he could look presentable. Then there is the case when Mr. Harvey spoke about the many times his car served as his hotel room because whatever money he made doing comedy wasn't enough to both take care of his children and sleep somewhere fancy.

In the beginning, these men didn't have the recognition they have now. However, they committed to the work assigned to them. Bishop was preaching and teaching to win souls and change lives, while some other preachers and pastors were more focused on receiving the finer cars, homes, and clothes. In entertainment, you're easily exposed to the world of alcohol and drugs and the ability to earn a lot of money. Mr. Harvey could have chosen that path, but he remained dedicated to the calling on his life to make people laugh. Before getting to where they are today, I am sure they had many questions regarding their obstacles and wondered if their time would ever come. Bishop Jakes could have decided to stop preaching or found other means to make his life easier or different, and likewise, with Mr. Harvey.

Caught between a rock and a blessing is all about decision-making. Usually, when the struggle is intense, it causes us to become anxious, and we try to achieve things before it's time.

However, in the latter part of Matthew 5:45, it says that "he gives his sunlight to both the evil and the good, and he sends rain on the just and the unjust alike." (NLT)

When I read that passage of scripture, I realized that it's not about if God is going to do it, but when. Everything is about God's timing. What God allows one individual to receive has no bearing on what or when another will receive. God didn't forget about any of us. Bishop Jakes and Mr. Steve Harvey, who continue to receive and the many others in line waiting their turn, will understand that there is pressure before the promise. Remember, before gold forms, it must go through a pressure process. The *process* scrapes off all infirmities.

The elder son needed to come to himself too. He was busy looking at what the father did and began feeling left out. I would even detect a bit of jealousy. When having their talk, the father told his elder son, all I have is yours because you have been with me. This teaches us not to become upset with those who seemingly receive blessings without going through or committing to anything. We cannot

Joyce Y. Lemmon

become fixated on "the haves and have nots." The father reassured his eldest son that his faithfulness had earned him an inheritance. Ephesians 1:11 says, "Furthermore, because we are united with Christ, we have received an inheritance from God, for he chose us in advance, and he makes everything work according to his plan." (NLT)

If we stay with God, our inheritance is sure. The father knew the strength of his eldest son and the weakness of the younger. In this scenario we must remember that it's not what we think, and the other person's issues are not about us. Get past it! Trust God and know that whatever he promised us is for us. Stay faithful and stay committed to the task that God has assigned. Here are a few more wisdom nuggets.

1. Don't look at what the other person is doing.
2. When you are into yourself, your circumstances take over, but when you come to yourself, you overtake the circumstances.
3. Come to yourself and trust God.

CHAPTER SIX

THROW YOUR NET BACK IN

Luke 5:3-5 – He climbed into the boat that was Simon's and asked him to put out a little from the shore. Sitting there, using the boat for a pulpit, he taught the crowd. When he finished teaching, he said to Simon, "Push out into deep water and let your nets out for a catch." Simon said, "Master, we've been fishing hard all night and haven't caught even a minnow. But if you say so, I'll let out the nets." (MSG).

We have often been in situations where we fasted and prayed for something and didn't receive the expected blessing in a specified time. The minister extended an invitation to come to the altar. They prayed with us and told us to hang in there. We stood in agreement, and still no results. Days turned into weeks that turned into months, turned into years, and still, nothing happened. So, what do you do when you feel like your prayers have gone unanswered, or God has forgotten about you? You need to throw your net back in.

My Personal Application

I remember when the ministry began in 1996, and we were sharing a building in Brooklyn, New York. One day while at work, the Lord spoke and had me draw a picture of what our church would look like. Please understand, I didn't know how to draw, but I began to as the Holy Spirit guided me. Upon completion, I folded the paper and placed it inside my Bible. I carried this drawing around for about two years.

One night while leaving school at the Bible Institute I was attending, I picked up the Love Express newspaper to see a building was for rent in Queens. It was late in the evening, but the Holy Spirit told me to call the number listed. Because of the hour, I didn't think anyone would pick up and decided to wait until morning. However, the Holy Spirit gave an extra nudge to call, and I did. To my surprise, someone answered. We made an appointment for the following morning. The next day when I arrived at the building and went inside, I saw a sanctuary identical to the drawing I carried for at least two years. I knew it was the building God was giving us. I had no clue how the ministry would afford it, but I knew the property was ours.

The process of trying to obtain a mortgage was difficult and time-consuming. The building owner needed to move swiftly because he was contracted to purchase another building for his ministry. As time went on, I began thinking maybe I was wrong about purchasing. Perhaps the building the Lord had for me wasn't that one, but I held on to what I believed.

After waiting a few months for loan approval, the owner called me stating that he couldn't wait any longer. He had to sell the building, and another person was interested and ready to pay cash. Well, I was devastated, but told him I understood. When I hung up the phone, the tears began falling. I didn't know how to tell the ministry we couldn't get the building. Then I heard a voice say, pray again. Like Simon, I felt I didn't need to pray anymore because the owner said he could no longer wait on us to get the loan. But the voice said pray again. So, I went into another office, closed the door, and began to pray. I remember thanking God for the opportunity.

I told God that if that building was not the one, I knew he had another one for me somewhere. I wiped my tears and went back to work. The very next day, while at work, the owner called to tell me that the Lord said the building was to be mine. He could not sell it to anyone else. He asked if it was possible for us to pay rent until we could get a mortgage. Immediately, I said yes and met with him that Saturday to get the keys. I received the blessing God had for me by throwing my net of prayer back in.

The opening of Luke chapter five states, while preaching on the shore of the Sea of Galilee, Jesus saw two ships by the lake, but the fishermen had gone to wash their nets. Jesus entered one of the ships belonging to Simon and asked him sail out a little from the land where he began to teach the people from the ship. Upon completing his teaching, Jesus instructs Simon to go further into the deep and throw his net back into the water for a catch. This may remind you of the times when you prayed, fasted, praised, or worshipped and felt it was to no avail. Then you hear the spirit of the Lord telling you to pray, fast, praise, or worship again. If you are honest, you probably responded, Lord, I did that already, and it didn't work. That is what Simon said in a manner of speaking. Simon said to Jesus, we have toiled (worked hard) all night and caught nothing.

The Revelation

In 1 Kings 18:41, Elijah told Ahab that there was a sound of the abundance of rain. In verses 43-44, Elijah told his servant to look towards the sea, but his servant reported seeing nothing. The Prophet then told the servant to go again the seventh time. That information shows us the servant had already gone six times with nothing to report. The servant, like many of us, probably became a little frustrated from the six times he went as the prophet said and saw nothing. Doesn't this remind you of the times you gave God your all and felt like you received nothing in return? Elijah said go again the seventh time. Frustrated or not, the servant went, and the last time, he saw something. The scripture declares that he saw a cloud rising out of the sea, and he saw a man's hand. In the case of Simon, tired and probably a little frustrated, said to Jesus, "nevertheless, at thy word, I will throw my net back in." In verse six, when Simon threw the net back in, he caught a multitude of fish until the net began breaking. He gathered so many fish until the fishermen nearby had to come to help him before the ship sank.

I know I said this before, but the enemy desires to frustrate us until we become fearful and want to give up. Simon could have chosen to go home after working all night and catching no fish. His attitude was justified if he said, "I've done that already." He was caught between going home after having a non-eventful evening or listening to Jesus' instructions. His obedience of throwing the net yielded the results hoped for. When the servant of Elijah went the seventh time, there came a tremendous downpour of rain. God can do the impossible when your situation looks bleak.

Jesus is telling us to throw our net back in. Throw your praise back and worship back in because there's a multitude of blessings in the next catch.

CHAPTER SEVEN

SPEAK LIFE AND ENCOURAGE YOURSELF

1 Samuel 30:6 – "And David was greatly distressed; for the people spoke of stoning him, because the soul of all the people was grieved, every man for his sons and his daughters; but David strengthened himself in the Lord his God." (NKJV)

Imagine returning home after being away for some time and finding your loved ones and possessions missing. Someone has invaded your space and stolen everything important to you. You are angry and afraid. Angry because someone had the audacity to invade your privacy, and fearful because you have no idea what would happen to your loved one or if something has already happened to them. Well, this was David's situation.

When David returned from battle, he discovered that the Amalekites had invaded the south and burned Ziklag with fire. In addition, the women and children of David and his men were taken captive, which caused them to cry out and weep until they became weak. Though David's family was taken along with the families of his men, he was blamed, and the people wanted to stone him. The outcry of his men and the desire to kill him caused great distress upon David. I am sure he felt like his back was against the wall and probably thought how he would get through it. David was caught between his anger and grief and the anger and grief his men had towards him. Caught in a dilemma where there was no one to encourage David, he had to encourage himself.

We cannot always look to others for help or rely on those not going through a situation themselves. In some cases, as soon as you begin to tell someone about your troubles, instead of trying to encourage and help you, they start telling you about theirs. David's men were in no position to help him or give advice on what to do. They were too distraught to think clearly, and they wanted to kill their leader. Therefore, David had to find his strength. So, what did David do? He did what we, especially leaders, do when caught in situations where everyone is looking to us for the answer or solution. David went to the Lord and asked, "Shall I pursue after the troops?" In other words, do I stay here, or do I go and retrieve what belongs to me?

David's ability to encourage himself and inquire of the Lord gave him a great victory. Often, we feel defeated because of negative self-talk and listening to others who discourage us. For example, have you ever discussed a plan you had with a "supposed friend," and they never gave you a vote of confidence, but instead, they pointed out every possible way you could fail? Or maybe there was a time you thought you could be successful at something, but fear overtook you to the point of pushing your thoughts or dreams to the side? Well, this is the time when you should become your own inspiration and hope.

My Personal Application

Speaking life and personal encouragement helped me write this book. I began penning over twelve years ago but became discouraged because I didn't think it would be any good. For many years I had low self-esteem. I never believed in myself because not many people ever encouraged me to believe in me. Knowing that life and death are in the power of the tongue, I had to inspire, hope, stimulate and believe in myself. Most importantly, I had to believe God would help me. Like David, I asked God, should I go after it. The Lord said to me, go after it. Romans 8:37 reminded me that "But in all things we overwhelmingly conquer through Him who loved us." And Philippians 4:13 rings in my ear that "I can do all things through him who strengthens me." (NASB)

The Revelation

There will be times when we'll face difficult situations that will require us to make decisions when our backs are against the wall. In these cases, we may look to others for assistance, and they can't offer any. If this happens and you are indecisive or confused, begin to speak life and inspire yourself. There is a song by Donald Lawrence that says, 'speak over yourself, encourage yourself, in the Lord.' Keep speaking life until you get the results you desire. Speak God's word and believe it no matter how you're feeling. Moreover, use His word to claim victory. Yes, you may feel like you are caught between that rock and a blessing. You may wonder what the outcome will be. Fear may rear its ugly head and discourage you from completing your assignment.

Though David's life was threatened, in the end, he received great victory. When he encouraged himself and asked the Lord what he should do, he found and destroyed the enemy recovering everything stolen from him and his men. Do not ever let anything or anyone deter you from what the Lord has told you to pursue. When the enemy says you cannot, speak life and encourage yourself because according to Proverbs 18:21a, "the tongue can bring death or life, and you shall eat the fruit thereof."

CHAPTER EIGHT

WHEN GOD BLINDS YOUR ENEMIES

2 Kings 6:18 – "When the Arameans attacked, Elisha prayed to God, "Strike these people blind!" And God struck them blind, just as Elisha said." (MSG)

Here again, we see a planned attack against the people of Israel. The King of Syria decided to war against them and held a meeting with his counsel to discuss the plan and to determine where the location of attack would happen. Like times before, Israel became fearful of what they heard and didn't know which way to go or what to do. Like most times, God stepped in and intervened on their behalf.

Through his Prophet Elisha, God revealed the enemy's plan and sent a message to the King of Israel. God said whatever way or place he was planning to

Caught Between a Rock and a Blessing

travel, not to pass that way because the enemy would be waiting to launch his attack. This reminds me of the times I've traveled and desired to go in one direction. That soft, still voice would tell me to go a different route. To me, the alternate road was much longer. However, each time I didn't listen and went the way I wanted, there was either an accident or heavy traffic causing a delay in reaching my destination.

The Prophet Elisha warned the King of Israel of Syria's plan so many times until the King of Syria thought he had a snitch in the camp. In verse 11, he called his officers together to find out who was the traitor informing Israel's King of his plans. He had only spoken to his counsel concerning the matter within the privacy of his bedroom. This should tell everyone that God knows what is going on, even in the secret of your bedroom. Neither our enemy nor we can hide anything from God. When they discovered Prophet Elisha revealed his plans, the King of Syria wanted to know where he was so he could capture the prophet.

When the word came back to the King of Syria on the location of Elisha, he got his horses, chariots, and men together to launch his attack and take the city. This reminds me of the exit from Egypt when Israel escaped the hands of Pharaoh. He went after them in the same manner. The Hebrew children became afraid because they were caught between the enemy and their freedom on the other side of the Red Sea.

I believe this is probably how the servant of Elisha felt when he arose early the following day and looked outside only to see that the Syrians had surrounded the city and asked his master, "What shall we do?" In other words, how are we getting out of this situation? Isn't this how we react when we feel surrounded by the enemy with nowhere to go? It doesn't matter if you are a lay member or a part of the ecclesiastical staff, each of us faced situations wondering how we were supposed to get through or come out of it.

When fear started to set in with Elisha's servant, Elisha told him, "Don't worry about it. There are more on our side than their side." (vs. 16 – MSG) Elisha told his servant that regardless of how many troops he saw, they had more.

I just want to take a minute to proclaim that God is an army all by himself. Like the servant, we,

Caught Between a Rock and a Blessing

too, sometimes have those with us who do not see what we see. Apostle, Bishop, Pastor, or whatever your leadership title may be, do not become upset when those that follow you do not catch the vision and see what you see. Be like the Prophet Elisha and ask God to open their eyes that they may see.

When Elisha prayed for the eyes of his servant to be open, God did it. The first time he only saw the Syrian army. The next time, he saw the mountain full of horses and chariots of fire protecting Elisha. If we ask God to open the people's eyes that support and walk with us, the Lord will cause them to see.

The same way God can open our eyes to see, he can close the eyes of our enemy. After Elisha prayed for his servants' eyes to be open, he then prayed for God to blind the eyes of those against him. The enemy (Syrians) went to Elisha's location, but upon their arrival, they were hit with blindness. They stood next to whom they were looking for but couldn't see him. Elisha, after telling them they were going the wrong way, used their blindness to lead them to Samaria, where the King of Israel dwelt. The Syrian army became captive to the ones they sought to imprison.

This is what happens when God blinds your enemy. Like Joseph said to his brothers in Genesis 50:20a, "You intended to harm me, but God intended it all for good." (NLT)

My Personal Application

In 1978 while attending a college in Brooklyn, I took a course entitled Secondary Education Part One. Until taking this course, I never had a problem completing papers. I never received a grade lower than a B. However, in this course, every paper I turned in came back with a D or F. According to the professor's comments, either there wasn't enough substance, or the information wasn't relatable to the subject matter. Even when I attempted to correct it, something was always wrong. The course was eight credits, and I couldn't afford to fail. I didn't know what I was doing wrong and felt attacked.

One day, I asked another student who received an A on all her papers to hold one of her assignments. I compared her writing and the piece I turned in, and there was no significant difference between the two. I couldn't understand why she had a passing grade, and I had a failing one. I had to do something. So, I copied the other student's paper who received an A, and I made a few changes. When I got the assignment back, I received another D. Not knowing what to do, I prayed and asked God to help me. I needed someone to listen to me, so I went to the head of the department and shared what happened. I even admitted to them that I copied another student's paper and still received a failing grade.

The department head immediately called the professor and questioned the professor's actions who didn't see that coming and was completely blinded by my experiment. The professor had no idea I would pursue this matter by going to the department head. I never knew or understood the motive. I do know that the professor never realized my paper was actually another student's. Because of this, they could not fail me from the class. God will make your enemy see what he wants them to see.

When we feel attacked, panic usually causes us not to see properly. We become so fixated on the enemy's capabilities, and we fail to see what God can do. We feel trapped with nowhere to go, and we automatically determine that the result will be unfavorable. I, however, encourage you as I encourage myself. Keep your eyes open. Ask God to open your eyes so that you can see but close the eyes of your enemies that they might not see. At all times, we must keep our eyes open and follow God, knowing that he will not let the enemy get but so close.

Psalm 27 was my mother's favorite scripture, and after reading it for myself, it wasn't long before it became one of my favorites. In the KJV of Psalm 27:1-2, it says, "the Lord is my light and my salvation whom shall I fear? The Lord is the strength of my life of whom shall I be afraid? When the wicked, even mine enemies and my foes came upon me to eat up my flesh, they stumbled and fell."

The Revelation

As I stated before, this Psalm is one of my favorite scriptures because I find it to be a great encouragement. Reciting it gives me inner strength and reminds me I can make it through whatever situation I face. So, when I interpret this Psalm, it goes something like this:

The Lord is my way to see and my deliverance from bondage. Why should I be afraid? If I can see, then I can escape bondage. The Lord is my source of power and energy, and there is no one for me to be afraid of. As long as I plug into my source, I don't have to be fearful of anyone. When those who are morally evil, vicious, sinful, or harmful or those who desire to launch an attack against me and the unfriendly and hostile intend to devour and destroy me, God will blind you, and you will trip trying to find me.

The enemy and his imps may have a plan to overtake you and wonder why they cannot touch you. It is because, like Job, there is a hedge around you. I can never say that the enemy will stop trying because he won't. However, I encourage you to keep your eyes wide open and ask God to keep the eyes of your enemy closed.

Psalm 91:1 – "He who dwells in the secret place of the Most High shall abide under the shadow of the Almighty." (NKJV)

The enemy may plan for your fall but continue to live in the shelter of God's protection. Find rest in him, for God will always intervene and cause your enemy to go blind.

CHAPTER NINE

EVERYBODY CAN'T GO

Judges 7:4 – "But the Lord told Gideon, There are still too many! Bring them down to the spring, and I will test them to determine who will go with you and who will not." (NLT)

What are destiny and destination? Webster defines destiny as a predetermined course of action, and destination is defined as an act of appointing, setting aside for a purpose.

Paraphrasing Ephesians 1:11, the Apostle Paul tells us that we were predestined to become recipients of an inheritance. It's not by chance or coercion that we come to have faith in God. Paul says we were intentionally chosen to have a purpose before the foundation of the world. So, this indicates to me that from the beginning, God not only had us on his mind, but God had a plan to endow us with purpose and destiny. We know this to be accurate based on Genesis 1:26 that says, "God spoke: Let us make human beings in our own image, make them reflect our nature, so they can be responsible for the fish in the sea, the birds in the air, the cattle, and yes, Earth itself, and every animal that moves on the face of the Earth." (MSG) We were destined to rule.

Sometimes when trying to obtain a goal or pursue our destiny, we feel we should incorporate others to assist us in the process. At times we organize a team of individuals who we think will assist in fulfilling the purpose God has for us. This is not necessarily the case. Sometimes incorporating various individuals tend to become a hindrance instead of an asset. Everyone who may have started with you may not finish with you. Everybody cannot go! Like trying to complete a jigsaw puzzle, the piece may look like it belongs, but when you try to place it in that spot, it doesn't fit.

Think back to when you first began your ministry. There were probably those who started with you and professed to never leave you. Today, they are no longer there. Those who left the ministry are not necessarily a bad thing. Neither is it any fault of yours. God sometimes assigns individuals to accompany you for a season. He already knew who was needed at that time and when their season would end. Those moments may prove to be a little painful, but I have come to understand that there are some roads we must travel without certain individuals. There are those who God allows to stay, and then there are those who God removes to fulfill our purpose and reach our destiny.

My Personal Application

Some years ago, I preached a message entitled, "One size does not fit all" and, I used clothing as an example. There are some articles of clothing like hosiery that has one size fits all on the package. However, factually, it doesn't fit all. A woman who may be tall and slender cannot wear the same size as a shorter and thicker woman. I remember buying a pair of hosiery like that. When I tried to put them on, they did not fit properly because they were too short.

Another example I used was women who had the same shoe size. Having the same shoe size doesn't mean we can wear an identical or exact type of shoe because one may have a wide foot, another may have a narrow foot, and another may have a medium foot. All three wear the same size, but not all three can wear each other shoes.

When Deliverance Tabernacle began, there was excitement and enthusiasm. Each week various individuals attended and told us what a great time they had. Several received Christ in their life and joined the ministry. There were services where we had to find seats to accommodate the congregation. As the years went by, the ministry became older, and things changed. Our financial obligations increased, and we had more responsibilities to maintain the building. To be honest, there were times when the ministry struggled, but not everyone could handle the pressure. Though individuals left for various reasons, I learned how never to take it personally. In ministry, some prefer megachurches, and some desire the smaller personal setting. Some people welcome change and new directions. There are those who never like change or new direction. Leaders never take it personally when people leave the ministry. Everyone won't fit in with God's plan.

Joyce Y. Lemmon

Now, you may wonder what does this have to do with being caught between a rock and a blessing. Or what does it have to do with being afraid and wondering how you will get through a situation? Again, think back to when you first began your ministry.

1. You became dependent on some of those individuals who had been with you for a significant amount of time.
2. You trusted and became comfortable with them.
3. Everything appeared to be going well with the ministry, its growth, and with the finances.
4. You're the visionary who received instructions from the Lord, pointing you in a different direction.
5. One or two people that have been with you from the beginning may not grasp the new vision and direction God's given you.

Let me remind you that these are the same ones who said they would never leave and would follow you as you follow Christ. You, the leader, are fully aware that you must follow God. However, there is that little part on the inside that tugs and says, "You do not want to lose that faithful member." If you're not careful, you may compromise what God has instructed partly because you're unsure how you would make it if they left. When you become dependent on people like this, you may even second guess hearing God correctly or question whether you made the right decision. The bottom line is we must adhere to God's instructions. If that means people leaving, then let them because everybody can't go.

The Revelation

As we look at Gideon, he was given the assignment to rescue the people of Israel from the hands of the Midianites and Amalekites. According to scripture, Gideon had 32,000 men in his army to defeat the enemy. In Gideon's mind, this was probably more than enough men to complete the job. However, the Lord spoke and informed him that the army's size was too large. Gideon took 10,000 men instead and was probably still confident in winning the battle and completing his assignment until the

Lord told him to reduce the army's size again. This time the Lord reduced the size of the army to 300 men. Now, if I were Gideon, I would have had a thousand questions to ask the Lord. My main question would be: How can I effectively complete this assignment with such a significant reduction?

If you read the entire story concerning Gideon, you would find that the first reduction resulted from the Lord telling Gideon that if he let all 32,000 go to fight, the people (Israel) would take the credit for the victory. In the second reduction, God needed to see who was paying attention and who would be alert. Only 300 of those men qualified. It only took 300 men to defeat 135,000.

I believe we all desire growth and success within our ministries. When members leave, we may not understand why. I know that early in my ministry when someone left, I wrecked my brain trying to figure out why and what happened. There were even times when I called them personally asking them to return, and they never did. Did it hurt? Yes! I thought we had a good thing going. But then God gave me inner peace. He began to show me, the person or persons were only there for a season. They served the purpose God had for them for that period and weren't assigned to go all the way. They could only go as far as God allowed.

When my mother began teaching me how to cross the street, she started by walking me to the corner of the street and instructing me to look for the green light (safe to walk) and the red light (stop and wait). Once the light turned green, she would stand there until I reached the other side. After a few weeks, my mother wanted to see how I would do on my own and decided not to walk with me one morning. I wasn't comfortable with her decision. I knew eventually I had to do it alone. I was getting older, and I needed to learn how to cross the street independent of her. Though I may have desired for my mother to walk with me a little longer, I came to understand that she had taken me as far as she could.

Our purpose and destiny are not based on who we think should accompany us. It is based on who God says should accompany us. Keep in mind that you may have to travel this road alone. Stop thinking to achieve goals or reach destiny everything needs to be done on a grand scale. Can a large membership help you obtain some of the things you need? Yes, but with the right group, the same goals can be achieved with a smaller membership. When God gives you an assignment, don't worry about the quantity of who you have. Instead, trust God for the quality of those you have. Take who God tells you to take and leave who God tells you to leave because everybody can't go.

CHAPTER TEN

JUST WAIT

Psalm 27:14 – "Wait for the Lord; Be strong, and let your heart take courage; Yes, wait for the Lord." (NASB)

Often, we take matters into our own hands rather than patiently wait for the Lord's response to our prayers. The Merriam-Webster Dictionary states that waiting is to "remain inactive but in readiness or expectation." This means that as I wait for God to give me a clear course of action, I remain ready and expect to receive what he has for me.

When waiting on God, as I stated several times in this book, the enemy will use the time to get you off-track and lose focus. Remember fear complicates in hopes of causing the believer to abort their faith.

As I stated previously, the enemy wants you to fearfully wait. As believers, we must understand that inactivity or waiting doesn't mean we do nothing. Remaining inactive while waiting on God means we shouldn't interfere with his plan or become impatient with him by coming up with our own course of action. Instead, we remain active in keeping our faith and trusting until the promise is manifested.

Acts 1:4-5 – "And being assembled together with them, He commanded them; not to depart from Jerusalem, but to wait for the Promise of the Father, which, He said, you have heard from Me; for John truly baptized with water, but you shall be baptized with the Holy Spirit not many days from now." (NKJV)

My Personal Application

When I received my driver's license at age 20, the first thing I wanted to do was purchase myself a car. Every morning I looked in the newspaper to see if anyone was selling one within my budget. Finally, I read someone was selling a 1974 Chevy Vega. Now, both my father and uncle told me not to buy that car because it had an aluminum engine, and it would give me trouble. Additionally, the car was a stick shift, and I did not have any experience driving that type of vehicle. However, I was determined to look at the car. My dad and uncle took me to see it, and I loved it mainly because it was red, my favorite color. I couldn't test drive it because I had no experience operating a stick shift. My father and uncle told me to wait and see if someone was selling a car more reliable. However, despite the warning, it was in my budget and my favorite color, so I purchased the car anyway.

By the end of the week, I learned how to drive a stick and was all smiles. By week two or three, my husband drove the car. One day on his way back home, the car began smoking. All you could see was this thick black smoke coming from the exhaust. The pretty red car I had for about one month needed a transmission. My father and uncle looked at me and said, I told you to wait. All I had to do was continue to check the newspaper and hold on to my money until the right vehicle came along. I should have waited!

Remember the story of Abraham and Sarah. A prophecy came in their old age; Sarah would con-

Caught Between a Rock and a Blessing

ceive and give birth to the promised son. We know that this event did not occur overnight because all things are done in God's timing. Instead of trusting God, the spirit of impatience and fear crept in, and Sarah and Abraham decided to help God out. Please understand that GOD DOES NOT NEED OUR HELP!

How many times have we said that we trust God, knowing everything takes place in due season but turned around and took charge? How many times did we complain and said that we could not take a situation any longer and did things our way only to regret it? It was more times than you or I probably care to mention.

In fear of believing the prophecy that Abraham would receive the promised heir would not happen, Sarah and Abraham handled it. Sarah encouraged Abraham to lay with her maidservant, which resulted in the birth of Ishmael. This impulsive act brought about anger and jealousy between Sarah and Hagar. Results don't go as planned when we take matters into our own hands. Waiting and being in the place of readiness is necessary. Usually, when we interfere, we mess things up. Hagar didn't need to be given to Abraham to bring forth an heir.

The scripture tells us " –Be careful (anxious) for nothing; but in everything by prayer and supplication with thanksgiving let your request be made known unto God" (Philippians 4:6), which simply means pray, give thanks, and do not worry about anything.

Being hasty and impatient is not the key to receiving your heart's desire. As believers, we cannot attempt to negotiate the terms of our destiny with God regardless of how difficult our situations may seem.

At the appointed time, Abraham and Sarah did receive God's promise in the birth of their son Isaac. They never inquired of the Lord when they began to feel anxious and uncertain. Instead, they came up with their plan, which added more anxiety and pressure to an already difficult situation. Implementing your own ideas can potentially go against God's plan and will cause more stress and uncertainty. The scripture in Isaiah 55:8 says, "My thoughts are nothing like your thoughts says the Lord. And my ways are far beyond anything you could imagine." (NLT) For some reason, we always think we know what is best for us. But God knows the way for us, and it is God who orders our steps and holds our destiny.

The call for me to preach began at eleven years old. I was excited and ready to do God's will. My mentor was the late Evangelist Martha Floyd who saw something in me. I had her full support. However, when I told my mother, who told my aunts, they decided I wasn't ready yet. As far as I was concerned, they didn't know what they were talking about. God called me to preach, and I needed to be preaching. The family told me to wait. I was a child, and I didn't have a choice or say in the matter. I couldn't understand why they were holding me back. I became angry, and rebelled.

As I got older, I did things I shouldn't have and mixed up with people I should have stayed away from. During this time of anger and rebellion, I continued to feel the Holy Spirit tugging at me. I finally realized my behavior was wrong and not acceptable to God, so I received Christ in my life for real. When God called me in 1989, that time, I was ready. I know now that if I had attempted to preach back in 1969, I would have wholly shipwrecked my life simply because I didn't wait. I needed to mature and learn God's word. Just because we desire to do a particular thing doesn't mean it's the right time to do it.

The Revelation

Waiting plays a significant role when you feel caught between a rock (the overwhelming situation) and a blessing (God's promise). You may experience fright or panic because you don't know how to get through while going through. As intense as this might be, do not take matters into your own hands. Don't do like I did when I wanted to preach the word too early or purchase a vehicle despite warnings. Wait until God gives you a clear course of action. Remain ready while expecting to receive what he has for you. Trust God because his promises are sure. Apply Psalm 27:14 (NASB), which tells us to wait for the Lord; be strong and let your heart take courage; Yes, wait for the Lord.

CONCLUSION

I pray you are encouraged to continue this journey regardless of what may come upon you. Life comes with tests and trials, and some will be easier to handle than others. What is being presented will undoubtedly appear frightening, but I encourage you not to be afraid.

When you were younger, do you remember going to the amusement park and wanting to go to the haunted house? Well, I remember going on an outing a long time ago, and my sisters Yvonne and Sheila wanted to go into the haunted house with me.

In the beginning, it wasn't too scary, but as we continued to walk through, the exhibits and scenes became more frightening. Suddenly, mummies and ghosts began to jump out in front of us, and we hollered and screamed.

At one point, when we were about halfway through, my sisters were too afraid to continue and

Caught Between a Rock and a Blessing

tried to go back, hoping to get out. However, the house wasn't set up that way. To get out or get through, you had to keep moving forward.

This probably reminds you of ministry when you first started. In the beginning, it didn't seem so hard, but as you continued, all types of situations jumped out at you. Some of it was rather frightening and possibly made you want to withdraw your 'Yes.' However, there's no retreating from ministry or the assignment God set up for you. So, move in a forward direction!

When I realized they were not walking with me but screaming and crying behind me, being the oldest, I went and pulled them along until we made it to the exit door. Guess what? There will be times when our brothers and sisters may become wedged between the cares of life and may not know how to move forward to get through. We may need to grab and pull them out. Again, you must move forward if you are going to get through. You cannot go back and never allow yourself to stay stuck in the middle.

David, a man after God's own heart, periodically experienced obstacles. I am pretty sure he often had to figure out how he would get through situations. In Psalm 23:4a, David said, "Even when the way goes through Death Valley, I'm not afraid." (MSG)

He recognized there would be times or moments of:

- facing intense darkness and danger
- being caught in the Death Valley

However, he was going to walk through and come out because, in the latter part of verse 4, David said, "when you walk at my side, your trusty shepherd's crook makes me feel secure." (MSG). Like David, who stood between the side of intense darkness and danger and the side of victory, we, too, are sometimes in that same place.

In a hymn entitled, "We are climbing Jacob's Ladder," there is a verse that says, "Every round goes higher and higher." Well, to go higher, we must keep climbing even when we feel caught between life situations and the promises of God. Climb when life throws a curveball. Climb even when we don't know what to do. Keep climbing

Caught Between a Rock and a Blessing

when we see obstacles on one side and the Lord's blessings on the other while being smack dab in the middle. When we feel caught between the circumstance or circumstances and the blessings of God, we can and will make it through. We will get out of the haunted house if we just keep going. That is how we are going to get through while going through.